Let Freedom Ring

Eli Whitney

American Inventor

by Katie Bagley

Consultant:
Ray Douglas Hurt, Ph.D.
Director, Graduate Program in Agricultural
History and Rural Studies
Iowa State University, Ames, Iowa

Bridgestone Books
an imprint of Capstone Press
Mankato, Minnesota

Bridgestone Books are published by Capstone Press
151 Good Counsel Drive, P.O. Box 669, Mankato, Minnesota 56002
http://www.capstone-press.com

Printed in the United States of America

Library of Congress Cataloging-in-Publication Data
Bagley, Katie.
    Eli Whitney: American inventor/by Katie Bagley.
    p. cm.—(Let Freedom Ring)
    Includes bibliographical references and index.
    Summary: A biography of the inventor of the cotton gin, whose application of
standardized parts to the production of weapons and other machines was a major
influence in the development of industry.
    ISBN 0-7368-1553-8 (hardcover)
    1. Whitney, Eli, 1765–1825. 2. Inventors—United States—Biography.
[1. Whitney, Eli, 1765–1825. 2. Inventors.] I. Title. II. Series.
TS1570.W4 B34 2003
609.2—dc21   2002011785

Editorial Credits
Kremena Spengler, editor; Karen Risch, product planning editor; Kia Adams,
series designer; Juliette Peters, book designer; Angela Gahler, illustrator; Kelly Garvin,
photo researcher

Photo Credits
Corbis, cover (inset), 31, 43 (bottom), Bettmann, 5, 35, Lester Lefkowitz, 41
Hulton Archive by Getty Images, 9, 39
Library of Congress, 32, 33, 37
National Archives, 27, 43 (top)
North Wind Picture Archives, 7, 10, 12, 15, 17, 19, 23, 24, 38
Stock Montage, Inc., cover, 21

1   2   3   4   5   6   08   07   06   05   04   03

Table of Contents

Chapter One

American Inventor

One evening in 1792, a 27-year-old New Englander named Eli Whitney listened to Georgia planters complain about the hard times. The South had no crops to sell for money. Cotton would grow in the South, but most cotton plants had seeds that were hard to remove. Until some machine could be invented to remove the seeds, cotton was little better than a weed.

Eli had just arrived in Savannah, Georgia. His friend Catherine Greene had invited him to stay at her farm, or plantation. Greene had already seen Eli's skill with tools. She believed he could make anything. Greene and her plantation manager, Phineas Miller, encouraged Eli to try to help the planters.

Eli Whitney developed the cotton gin in his workshop at Mulberry Grove plantation in Savannah, Georgia.

After months of experiments, Eli came up with a machine that solved the planters' problems. He made a tube covered with hooks that turned past a wire comb. When someone put freshly picked cotton onto the tube, it caught on the hooks. The hooks pulled the cotton through the comb, leaving behind the seeds. This machine was Eli's cotton gin. It worked so well that its design hardly ever changed.

Eli's Inventions Change the Nation

Eli's cotton gin changed the South. Before the cotton gin, few people were able to make money by growing cotton. After Eli's invention, cotton plantation owners could become rich. More Southern farmers began to grow cotton. Cotton became the South's most important crop.

Eli is most famous for inventing the cotton gin. But people also remember him for developing a system of mass production. Eli's system helped workers use machines to make the same parts over and over again. The parts were put together to make finished goods. Eli's system allowed workers to produce more goods more quickly.

Eli's cotton gin removed the seeds from cotton.

Chapter Two

Early Life and Education

Eli was born on December 8, 1765, in Westborough, Massachusetts. At that time, Massachusetts was still a British colony. Eli's father was a farmer. Eli had a younger sister and two younger brothers. His mother, Elizabeth Fay Whitney, died when he was young. Eli's father remarried when Eli was 13 years old.

Eli was curious about how things worked. When he was 8 years old, Eli took his father's watch apart and put it back together without anyone knowing. When he was 12 years old, he built a violin. Even though violins are difficult to make, Eli's violin sounded good.

Eli was also good at fixing things around the farm. He learned how to make horseshoes and other metal items. He set up a blacksmith shop on his father's farm.

When Eli was young, he set up a blacksmith's shop on his father's farm. This picture shows a blacksmith shaping metal in the 1790s.

In 1775, the Revolutionary War (1775–1783) began in nearby Concord, Massachusetts. Eli was too young to fight in the war, but he contributed in another way. Before the war, the colonists had imported nails and other goods from Britain. During the war, these goods were hard to find. Eli invented a machine to make nails. He made nails in his workshop and sold them to his neighbors. Eli's business was so successful that he had to hire another worker to help him.

When Eli was young, the Revolutionary War started in Concord, Massachusetts.

After the war, Eli made less money making nails. He simply switched to making hat pins and walking canes. But Eli had less time for his shop because he had to work more on his father's farm.

Eli Solves Problems

Eli worked hard in school but was an average student. He was a slow reader but was good at math. Eli wanted more education. He decided to go to Yale College in New Haven, Connecticut. Most Yale students studied law or religion, but Eli wanted to study science and engineering. Eli's family did not support his decision. They did not have money to pay for his education.

Eli did not let these problems stop him. He began teaching school in 1783 and taught until 1789. He saved his money. He studied for the Yale entrance exams. To get into Yale, students had to be able to read Latin and Greek. After he passed his exams, Eli entered Yale in 1789, at the age of 23. Eli was older than most other students.

At Yale, Eli learned about the newest experiments in science and studied the latest improvements in technology. Unlike most students, Eli spent more time studying how machines worked than reading books. Once, Eli repaired a broken machine for a professor who needed the machine to complete an experiment.

Eli entered Yale College in 1789. At Yale, Eli learned about the newest experiments in science.

"A Mechanic Spoiled"

When Eli was a student, he asked a workman at Yale College to lend him some tools. The carpenter did not trust a student to take care of them, but Eli finally talked him into lending the tools. The carpenter was impressed with Eli's mechanical skills. He exclaimed to Eli, "There was one good mechanic spoiled when you went to college."

Disappointment in Georgia

When Eli graduated in 1792, he could not find work that fit his talents. Few science or engineering jobs existed in Eli's time.

In 1792, Eli got a job offer as a private teacher for some children in South Carolina. He accepted the job and traveled to New York City. He planned to take a boat from New York City to Savannah and then go on to South Carolina. In New York City, Eli met Catherine Littlefield Greene. She was the widow of General Nathaniel Greene, a Revolutionary War hero.

When Eli arrived in Savannah, he found out that the teaching job would not pay enough for him to live. He was in a new state with no money. Fortunately, Greene invited him to stay at her Mulberry Grove plantation. She said Eli could live there and study law.

Mulberry Grove

Eli accepted Greene's offer and stayed at Mulberry Grove. He became friends with Phineas Miller. Miller had graduated from Yale a few years before Eli. He had moved to Georgia to teach General Greene and Catherine Greene's children. At the time Eli met him, Miller was the plantation manager. Later, Catherine Greene and Miller married.

Eli wanted to do something to thank Greene for inviting him to stay. He began to fix things around Mulberry Grove. He also invented devices to help the people who lived on the plantation. Greene once complained that her sewing frame was badly built and was tearing the fabric. Eli quickly made a new frame for her. He also created toys for her children. Greene and Miller thought highly of Eli's skills.

After college, Eli lived at Mulberry Grove plantation near Savannah.
Mulberry Grove was similar to the plantation shown in this picture.

Chapter Three

Inventing the Cotton Gin

In the 1790s, the most popular fabrics were made from cotton. Mills in Great Britain and in the New England area of the United States made cotton thread and fabric. Mill owners had a great demand for raw cotton. Southern planters began to grow cotton because they had ready buyers. The soil and climate in the South were good for growing cotton. Farmers could make a lot of money with this cash crop.

The planters had a hard time keeping up with the mills' need for cotton. Before planters could sell the cotton, slaves had to separate the fibers from the seeds. One kind of cotton had seeds that were easy to remove. But this long-staple cotton grew only on the Sea Islands of Georgia and South Carolina.

In the 1790s, mills made their most popular fabrics from cotton.

Greene Befriends Eli

Eli might not have been so successful in life without Catherine Greene's support. She introduced him to people and told them about his talents. After she told her guests that Eli could invent a machine to remove cotton seeds, she said to one of them, "I have accomplished my aim. Mr. Whitney is a very deserving young man, and to bring him into notice was my object. The interest which our friends now feel for him will, I hope, lead to his getting some employment to enable him to prosecute [continue] the study of law."

Almost everywhere else, only short-staple cotton would grow. Short-staple cotton had short fibers and sticky green seeds. The fibers stuck to the seeds and were hard to separate. A handworker could separate the seeds from only 1 pound (.45 kilogram) of cotton each day.

Creating the Cotton Gin

One night, Greene was entertaining several guests. A few of them were officers who had served with her husband in the Revolutionary War. Greene told them that Eli could invent a machine to clean the cotton. She showed her guests some of the things that Eli had invented for her.

Eli objected that he had never even seen a cotton plant in his life. Greene and Miller encouraged him to try anyway. Eli wanted to please them and finally agreed.

Eli watched how the slaves cleaned the cotton by hand. They held the seed in one hand and pulled out the cotton fibers with the other. Eli tried to build a machine to copy this action.

Before Eli invented the cotton gin, slaves held the cotton seed with one hand and pulled out the cotton fibers with the other. This museum photo shows the seeds and the clean cotton.

The Cotton Gin Is a Success

Eli's first attempts to make a cotton gin were not successful. He made a wire screen to strain the seeds. But the screen kept jamming. So, Eli tried again. He built his final model in only 10 days.

The new cotton gin was a tube covered with wire hooks. Eli fed the raw cotton onto the tube. The tube turned, and the fibers caught on the hooks. The hooks passed through a large iron comb and pulled the fibers through. The cotton seeds were too large to pass through the comb and stayed behind. A brush that turned four times as fast as the hook-covered tube cleaned the cotton fibers off the hooks. The brush prevented the machine from jamming.

In April 1793, Greene invited some planters to Mulberry Grove to see the cotton gin. She even built a shed to display Eli's invention. Greene and the other planters were very excited. With the gin, one person could do the job of 50 hand workers. People could operate the gin by hand, water power, or horse power. The planters decided to plant their fields with cotton right away, even though Eli had made only one machine.

Eli's cotton gin was a tube covered with wire hooks. As the tube turned, the cotton fibers caught on the hooks and separated from the seeds.

Chapter Four

Effects of the Cotton Gin

On March 14, 1794, Eli received a patent on his invention. A patent is a right that Congress gives to an inventor. It protects an inventor from competition. Eli's patent said that only Eli could make the cotton gin for 14 years. No one else could copy his idea.

Eli did not have the money to manufacture cotton gins. Eli and Phineas Miller decided to go into business together. Miller would give Eli the money to build a factory, and the two would share the profits from the cotton gin. They named their company Miller & Whitney. Eli moved back to New Haven, Connecticut, and built a cotton gin factory. Eli and Miller thought they would become wealthy from Eli's invention.

Eli and Miller decided not to charge planters a set price for the cotton gin. Instead, they charged royalties.

Eli, shown here as a businessman, obtained a patent and started a company to make cotton gins.

A royalty is a fee people pay to a patent owner for the right to use the invention. A royalty is often a share of the user's profits. In exchange for the cotton gin, Miller & Whitney would get two-fifths of the profits from the cotton.

The invention of the cotton gin increased cotton growing in the South. Slaves toiled in the fields, picking, baling, or ginning the cotton. Some cotton gins were operated by steam.

In His Own Words

"One man and a horse will do more than 50 men with the old machines. 'Tis generally said by those who know anything about it, that I shall make a fortune by it." — Eli Whitney, in a letter to his father

Eli and Miller's decision to charge royalties hurt their company. Many planters wanted to buy the machine itself rather than pay the royalties.

Eli could not make the cotton gins fast enough. In 1794, an illness called scarlet fever hit Connecticut, and many of Eli's workers fell sick. In 1795, a fire damaged his shop. Many planters were afraid they would not receive the cotton gins in time to harvest their cotton fields.

Trouble with the Patent

Even though Eli's invention had a patent, some people started to copy his design without paying royalties. The cotton gin was simple, so it was easy to copy. Other people had been trying to make a cotton gin at the same time as Eli was building his. Some of them produced their own machines that

In His Own Words

"An invention can be so valuable as to be worthless to the inventor." — Eli Whitney, disappointed that farmers copied his gin rather than paying royalties for its use

were similar to Eli's. Many planters bought the copies or other inventors' cotton gins.

Eli sued these planters for not respecting his patent. The planters often won the suits because the Southern judges were more friendly to the planters. The lawsuits cost a lot of money, and Miller & Whitney went out of business in 1797.

Eli Struggles On

For a while, Eli continued his lawsuits but finally settled by making an agreement with each state. The state government would pay him a certain fee, and Eli's cotton gin would be public property in that state. In 1802, South Carolina agreed to pay $50,000. This amount was only half of what Eli wanted to charge, but he had lost hope of getting more and accepted it anyway.

North Carolina, Georgia, and Tennessee also agreed to make cotton gin payments. They did not always pay Eli as much as they promised. In the end, Eli earned only $90,000 for his cotton gin. Most of this money went to pay for the lawsuits and his other debts. Eli thought that the cotton gin would make him rich, but he made almost no money from it.

In 1806, a judge finally passed a decision that protected Eli's patent. But the patent was to end in 1807. Eli asked Congress to let him keep the patent longer to make up for his losses. Congress refused to renew the patent. Eli got upset and never bothered to get patents for any of his later inventions.

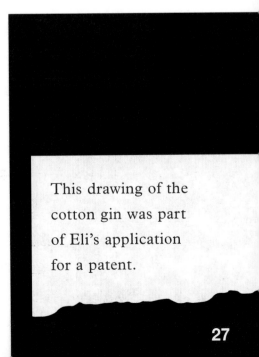

This drawing of the cotton gin was part of Eli's application for a patent.

The Gin Changes the South

Planters grew more and more cotton. In 1821, the South produced $20 million worth of cotton. By 1860, this amount had grown to $192 million. Cotton became the most important export in the country.

The South was the world's leading cotton producer. Planters shipped more and more cotton to Britain. New Orleans and other Southern port cities rapidly grew. The cotton gin made the planters rich.

Plantations began to spread west to increase cotton production. Planters moved to Alabama and Mississippi. They pushed the American Indians who were living there farther west or onto reservations.

Before the invention of the cotton gin, many people thought slavery would soon end. It cost planters to feed and clothe their slaves. Many people began to realize that holding people in slavery was cruel.

After the gin was invented, planters needed more slaves to grow, pick, and clean the cotton. The cotton gin made owning slaves economical. In 1790, fewer than 700,000 slaves lived in the United States. By 1850, nearly 4 million slaves lived in the country.

VIRGINIA

MISSOURI

NORTH
CAROLINA

TENNESSEE

INDIAN
TERRITORY

SOUTH
CAROLINA

ARKANSAS

MISSISSIPPI

TEXAS

ALABAMA

GEORGIA

LOUISIANA

FLORIDA

LEGEND

Cotton production
in 1820

Cotton production
in 1860

Chapter Five

The Uniformity System

Eli was almost broke after the cotton gin failed to make him rich. He needed to find a new way to earn money. He had an idea for a new manufacturing system.

In the 1790s, the U.S. government was afraid of a possible war against France. The government ordered new weapons and supplies for the military. It asked manufacturers to make guns called muskets. Eli claimed he could make 10,000 muskets in only two years. In 1798, he signed a contract with the government to make this large number of muskets.

In the 1700s, workers needed special skills to make a musket. A skilled worker known as an artisan made an entire musket from start to finish. He would form and fit each part especially for one musket. This process took several days.

In the 1700s, skilled workers known as artisans formed and fitted parts to make muskets.

If a part broke, the artisan had to make a new part to fit that one musket. Eli believed a faster way existed.

The System of Interchangeable Parts

Eli thought that an unskilled worker could make the same part over and over again. One worker would make only triggers. The triggers would match a model part and be exactly alike. Other workers would make other parts. Then someone would put the parts

Eli built this weapons factory at a place called Mill Rock near Hamden, Connecticut.

Whitney Arms

Eli had this advertisement printed for muskets he made under a contract with the U.S. government.

together. Any part could fit any musket. Eli called this system the uniformity system. Today, people call it the system of interchangeable parts.

Eli moved to Hamden, Connecticut, near New Haven. He built a factory for making weapons at a place called Mill Rock. This armory was located on the Mill River. The river provided water power for Eli's factory.

Eli created many machines to help workers make parts exactly alike. Workers could now produce more parts faster and with less training than an artisan had. Eli's system was the beginning of mass production.

Eli Shows Off His System

In 1801, Eli showed his system to Thomas Jefferson and other government officials. Eli sorted the parts for 10 muskets into separate piles. Then he chose one part from each pile and put them together to make a musket. He repeated his demonstration nine more times. The observers were amazed. Doubting officials were convinced.

Eli did not make 10,000 muskets in two years as he had promised. He needed more than 10 years to complete the contract. The government was patient because it wanted to help American manufacturers. Not long before, the country had won political independence from Great Britain in the Revolutionary War. The United States also wanted economic independence.

Eli was slow to complete his contract because he had to invent and build his machines. He designed a milling machine that allowed a worker to cut metal parts according to a pattern. The worker would clamp the metal to a workbench and fasten the pattern to the top. He then would use a metal wheel with sharp teeth to cut around the pattern, instead of using a chisel to cut the metal by hand. Eli probably did not invent the first milling machine, but his design was so good that people used it for more than 150 years.

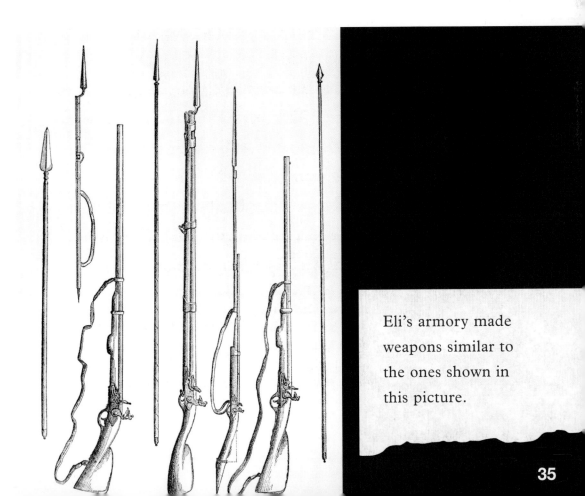

Eli's armory made weapons similar to the ones shown in this picture.

Chapter Six

The Later Years

For the rest of his life, Eli continued to manufacture weapons in Connecticut. Eli worked hard and made his employees work hard, too. Although he became wealthy, he always lived simply.

Eli built houses near the armory for his workers. He provided food for them and some training for their children. People called the workers' village Whitneyville. Before Eli got married, he lived in the village and cared for three of his young nephews.

Eli's letters to friends show that he felt lonely and wanted a family. In 1817, 51-year-old Eli married Henrietta Edwards. Edwards was the granddaughter of a famous New England minister named Jonathan Edwards. She was 31 years old. Eli and Henrietta had four children,

Eli built houses for his workers near his weapons factory.
The village became known as Whitneyville.

Frances, Elizabeth Fay, Eli Jr., and Susan. Susan died when she was only 21 months old. In the early 1800s, it was common for babies to die in childhood.

Eli became ill in 1822. He kept inventing things even while he was sick. On January 8, 1825, Eli died. His nephews and later his son, Eli Jr., took over the armory and continued to make weapons.

Workers used mass production to make bullets for guns in the 1870s.

Eli and the Industrial Revolution

Eli's cotton gin, milling machine, and system of mass production were part of the Industrial Revolution. The Industrial Revolution started in Great Britain during the late 1700s and spread through parts of western Europe and the United States in the early 1800s.

The Industrial Revolution brought huge changes to people's lives and work. Before the Industrial Revolution, workers made goods by hand. Most people worked at home on farms. During the Industrial Revolution, machines, like the sewing machine in this picture, replaced handwork. Machines greatly increased the production of goods. Factories developed as the places where machines and workers came together. Large numbers of people moved to the cities to work in factories. The Industrial Revolution changed the Western world from rural and agricultural to urban and industrial.

The Importance of Eli's System

Eli was not the first person to think of the system of interchangeable parts. Years before, some French gun makers were experimenting with a similar system. In the 1790s, Eli probably read reports of their work. But Eli proved that machines could be used to help workers produce the same parts. He taught people that mass production was possible.

Eli's system of interchangeable parts was a success. Other manufacturers copied his ideas. The system helped produce all sorts of goods. Manufacturers used Eli's system to make clocks, sewing machines, agricultural equipment, and tools. U.S. manufacturing became famous. British visitors to the United States thought highly of the uniformity system. They called it the American system.

Eli's success allowed others to follow. He helped make the United States a leading industrial nation. Eli's ideas were the first step to the assembly line. Manufacturers today still use the assembly line to make automobiles, televisions, computers, and other goods.

Manufacturers today still use Eli's system of interchangeable parts to produce goods on assembly lines.

TIMELINE

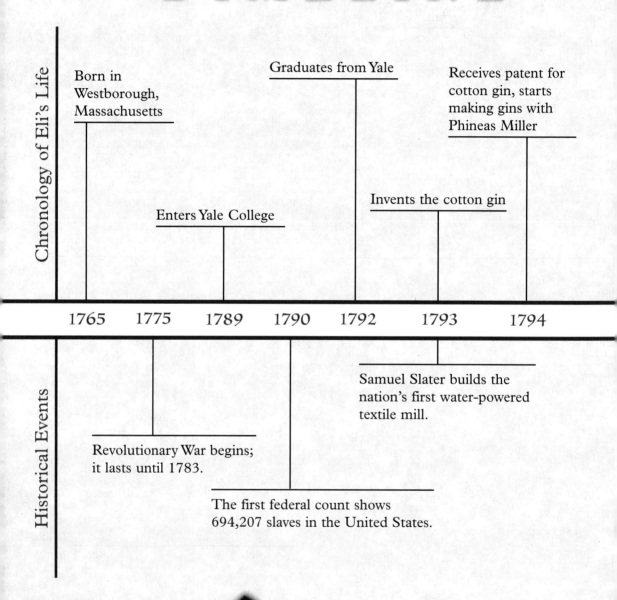

Chronology of Eli's Life

Born in Westborough, Massachusetts

Graduates from Yale

Receives patent for cotton gin, starts making gins with Phineas Miller

Enters Yale College

Invents the cotton gin

1765 1775 1789 1790 1792 1793 1794

Samuel Slater builds the nation's first water-powered textile mill.

Revolutionary War begins; it lasts until 1783.

The first federal count shows 694,207 slaves in the United States.

Historical Events

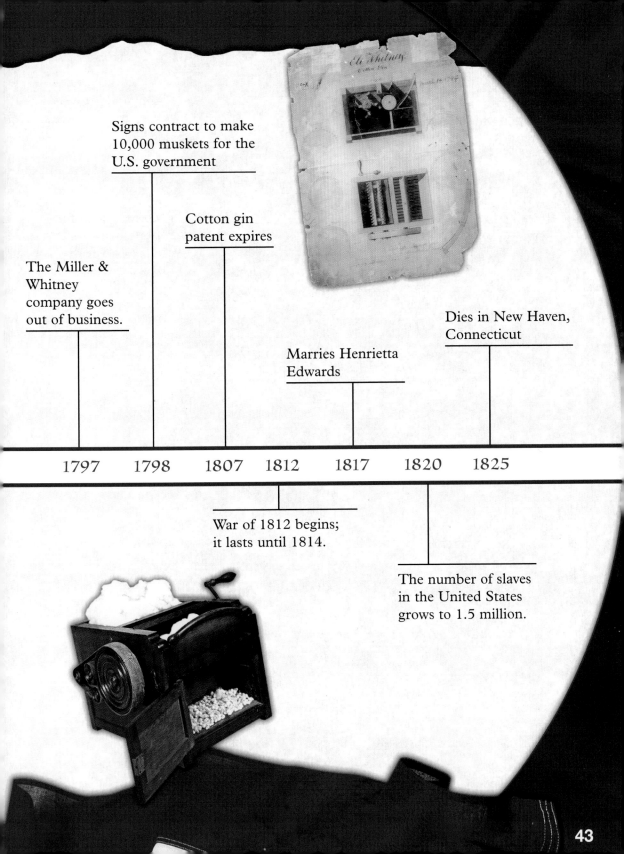

Signs contract to make 10,000 muskets for the U.S. government

Cotton gin patent expires

The Miller & Whitney company goes out of business.

Dies in New Haven, Connecticut

Marries Henrietta Edwards

| 1797 | 1798 | 1807 | 1812 | 1817 | 1820 | 1825 |

War of 1812 begins; it lasts until 1814.

The number of slaves in the United States grows to 1.5 million.

Glossary

armory (AR-mur-ee)—a factory that makes weapons

artisan (AR-tuh-zuhn)—a skilled worker, especially one whose occupation requires hand skill

interchangeable (in-tur-CHAYNJ-uh-buhl)—easily switched with something else

mass-produce (MASS pruh-DOOSS)—to produce goods in large quantity, usually by machinery

mill (MIL)—a building or group of buildings with machinery for making goods from raw materials

musket (MUHSS-kit)—a firearm once used by soldiers

patent (PAT-uhnt)—a legal document giving an inventor the right to to be the only person to make, use, or sell his or her invention for a certain number of years

plantation (plan-TAY-shuhn)—a large farm located in warm climates where crops such as coffee, cotton, or tobacco are grown

royalty (ROI-uhl-tee)—a payment to the owner of a patent for the right to use a device; sometimes a royalty is a share of the profit from the use of the device.

technology (tek-NOL-uh-jee)—science used to solve practical problems

For Further Reading

Bagley, Katie. *The Early American Industrial Revolution, 1793–1850.* Let Freedom Ring. Mankato, Minn.: Bridgestone Books, 2003.

Cefrey, Holly. *The Inventions of Eli Whitney: The Cotton Gin.* 19th Century American Inventors. New York: PowerKids Press, 2003.

Gaines, Ann. *Eli Whitney.* Discover the Life of an Inventor. Vero Beach, Fla.: Rourke Book, 2002.

Huff, Regan A. *Eli Whitney: The Cotton Gin and American Manufacturing.* The Library of American Lives and Times. New York: PowerKids Press, 2004.

St. George, Judith. *So You Want to Be an Inventor?* New York: Philomel Books, 2002.

Places of Interest

Eli Whitney Museum
915 Whitney Avenue
Hamden, CT 06517
Located in Eli's restored gun
factory, this museum has
programs and workshops that
teach about machinery and
technology. It includes an outdoor
water learning lab.

**National Inventors Hall of
Fame and Museum**
221 South Broadway
Akron, OH 44308-1505
The museum showcases
inventions from different ages and
offers hands-on activities for
would-be inventors.

**Westborough Historical
Society**
13 Parkman Street
Westborough, MA 01581
The society has information on
Eli's birthplace.

Internet Sites

Do you want to learn more about Eli Whitney?
Visit the FACT HOUND at *http://www.facthound.com*

FACT HOUND can track down many sites to help you.
All the FACT HOUND sites are hand-selected
by Capstone Press editors. FACT HOUND will fetch the best,
most accurate information to answer your questions.

IT IS EASY! IT IS FUN!
1) Go to *http://www.facthound.com*
2) Type in: 0736815538
3) Click on "FETCH IT" and
FACT HOUND will put you on
the trail of several helpful links.

You can also search by subject or book title. So, relax
and let our pal FACT HOUND do the research for you!

Index